Glimpses of the Divine II

With kind regards, ॐ *and prem*

Swami Niranjan

Glimpses of the Divine II

Sri Lakshmi-Narayana Mahayajna 2013

Yajna and satsangs held at Sannyasa Peeth, Munger, Bihar, India, from 7th to 12th September 2013

Yoga Publications Trust, Munger, Bihar, India

Published by Yoga Publications Trust
First edition 2014

ISBN: 978-93-84753-17-7

Publisher and distributor: Yoga Publications Trust, Ganga Darshan, Munger, Bihar, India.

Website: www.biharyoga.net

Printed at Aegean Offset Printers, Greater Noida

Dedication

In humility we offer this dedication to Swami Sivananda Saraswati, who initiated Swami Satyananda Saraswati into the secrets of yoga.

Contents

Introduction

This book is not simply a collection of inspiring satsangs and lessons on spiritual life, though you will find both here. In a greater sense, it is a celebration of faith, and every page offers the promise of peace, plenty and prosperity to anyone who reads it. The material contained herein signifies the unbroken succession of love, trust and devotion between the guru and disciple that lies at the heart of the Satyananda Yoga–Bihar Yoga Tradition and, more specifically, the tenet of Sannyasa Peeth.

In this second volume of *Glimpses of the Divine* we visit the third annual Sri Lakshmi-Narayana Mahayajna, a sublime spiritual gathering held at Sannyasa Peeth in Munger, Bihar. Held just weeks before the World Yoga Convention and the Bihar School of Yoga's Golden Jubilee Celebrations, this yajna was inspired by Swami Niranjanananda Saraswati. He called the time during which the yajna was held *Sumiran Saptah*, the week of remembrance: remembrance of God in the form of Narayana and remembrance of guru. For, it is only by the grace of guru that we may begin to glimpse the divine forces that exist all around us.

Throughout the week-long event, guru was the presiding energy in the hearts and minds of everyone present, while the presiding deities of Sannyasa Peeth's signature yajna were Lord Narayana and his consort, Ma Lakshmi, whose blessings were sought for sustenance, nourishment, preservation, and prosperity of the positive and the auspicious in life. Without basic prosperity, *poornata*, or complete fulfilment, can never be achieved. The Lakshmi-Narayana Mahayajna invokes these two cosmic forces to fulfil the third chapter in our guru's vision for human upliftment and awakening.

The seeds of Sannyasa Peeth were planted during the period that Sri Swami Satyananda spent in the ashram of his guru, Sri Swami Sivananda. A realized saint, Swami Sivananda taught integral yoga as a means to awaken the whole human being – from the intellect, to the emotions, to the physical actions, what he called the 'head, heart and hands' – and thus live the divine life. After leaving Swami Sivananda's ashram, Sri Swamiji all the while kept in mind his guru's vision.

The two great institutions that Sri Swamiji established during his lifetime indicate his unflinching commitment to that dream. The Bihar School of Yoga in Munger represents the seat for the development of the higher intellectual faculties, the 'head' of Swami Sivananda's threefold yogic vision. A yajna is conducted every year during Basant Panchami, BSY's Foundation Day, to propitiate Ma Saraswati, the goddess of higher knowledge. Rikhiapeeth, the ashram located in rural and impoverished Jharkhand, has become the home of the 'yoga of the heart'. The Cosmic Mother, who is the symbol of unparalleled service, love and selflessness, is invoked at the yearly Sat Chandi Mahayajna to ensure the success of Sri Swamiji's sankalpa of peace, plenty and prosperity for all.

Sannyasa Peeth is Sri Swamiji's final offering to his guru and was revealed to his spiritual successor, Swami Niranjan, shortly before he attained mahasamadhi in 2009. Inaugurated in 2011, Sannyasa Peeth is an innovative institution that uses the guiding principles of sannyasa and the guru-disciple relationship to draw out the individual's optimum creative expression in every action and within all areas of life. With this, the third and final installation, Swami Sivananda's 'hands', finally have a place to do their creative work.

The Sri Lakshmi-Narayana Mahayajna is conducted every year to fructify the vision of Sannyasa Peeth. The 2013 yajna was a grand affair, stretching out over an unprecedented eight-day period. Every moment of this marathon occasion was filled with special events: Swami Sivananda's birthday surprise from Lord Jagannath, the presence of Swami Satsangi, Srimati Krishna Devi's daily renderings of the Bhagavat Katha, the Ganesha Chaturthi pooja, and most importantly, the continuous, unbroken remembrance of guru, Lakshmi and Narayana through song, dance, storytelling and heartfelt celebration, bringing the light of the divine into every heart and mind.

It is not possible to recreate all the details of this event within the pages of a small booklet, but it is our sincere hope that this collection of satsangs and images aptly captures its essence, so that those who attended it may relive the blessings and prasad of the Sri Lakshmi-Narayana Mahayajna; and those who are experiencing it for the first time through this book can catch a glimpse of the beauty and magic of its precious days.

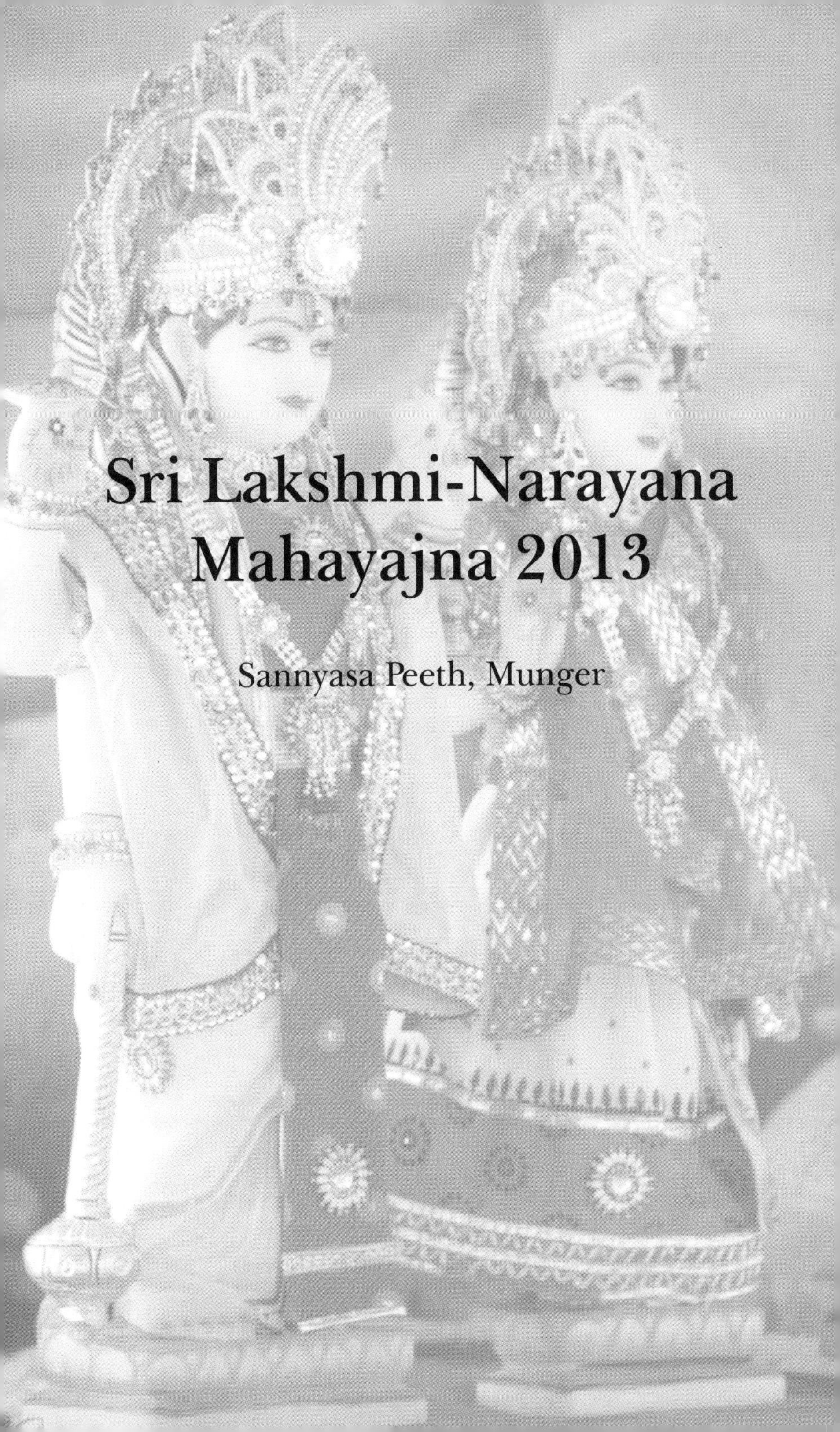

Sri Lakshmi-Narayana Mahayajna 2013

Sannyasa Peeth, Munger

Preparing for Divine Grace

Swami Niranjanananda Saraswati
7 September 2013

The program for the Lakshmi-Narayana Mahayajna started on the 5th and will go on until the 13th. We are calling this continuous program *Sumiran Saptah*, the week of remembrance. The 5th, the first day, is the commemoration of Sri Swami Satyananda Saraswati's attainment of mahasamadhi, and to remember our guru on the occasion of his mahasamadhi, a Sri Rudrabhisheka was performed. On the 6th, he was given bhu samadhi, and to remember him on the day of his bhu samadhi, the Sri Yantra Abhisheka was performed.

Tomorrow the Lakshmi-Narayana Mahayajna will start. The Lakshmi-Narayana Mahayajna is a yajna dedicated to Lord Narayana and Mother Lakshmi. Narayana is the sustainer of the universe, and Lakshmi is the symbol of prosperity and wealth, which is both material and spiritual. Since 2011, this Lakshmi-Narayana Mahayajna has been conducted here at Paduka Darshan, as per the command given by Sri Swamiji before his mahasamadhi. This invocation of Lakshmi-Narayana is his blessing to Sannyasa Peeth. The yajna is a blessing to Sannyasa Peeth, inspired by him and held under his direction.

Since the yajna started, people who have participated in this program have been witness to many extraordinary events and have been the recipients of grace, which has touched and beautified their life in many ways.

Role of the trinity

In Indian mythology there is the trinity of Brahma, Vishnu and Shiva. Brahma is the creator, Vishnu is the preserver, and Shiva is the destroyer, the changer. In the sannyasa tradition, as sannyasins we are followers of Shiva, yet our greeting is that of Narayana. *Hari Om* is a greeting of Narayana; *Namo Narayana* is a greeting of Narayana; however, the dress and tradition is that of Shiva. Thus, in this tradition of sannyasa, there is an integration of both the Narayana and the Shiva aspects; Shiva to bring change, and Narayana to sustain and maintain the positivity and beauty that Shiva has brought into life. Therefore, in Indian mythology, Shiva and Narayana complement each other. They do not oppose each other; rather, they complement each other and each one is a devotee of the other. Narayana is a devotee of Shiva, as Narayana seeks change in order to bring stability, and Shiva is a devotee of Narayana since Shiva is the changer and he seeks stability. They both represent two sides of the same coin.

From the religious point of view, people may say that they are different; from the spiritual point of view they are the same. That is how you have to look at them and that is how you have to understand them in your life as well. They are not separate from your life; they are experiences in your life that flower when your mind has crossed a milestone in its evolution.

Make a plan and follow it

Have you ever thought about your evolution, the milestones that you have reached? What is the milestone of your growth? Have you ever checked how much you have progressed, how much distance you have covered and how many more miles you have to go? This is important. Understanding the philosophy of Narayana and the philosophy of Shiva gives a clear picture of the milestones that you have travelled and the milestones that need to be covered.

The Lakshmi-Narayana Mahayajna is dedicated to Narayana, which is the nurturing aspect, the sustaining aspect. You can plan many things in life, however, if you do not adhere to what you have planned, then all your planning comes to zero. When you adhere to a plan and follow a system, a path and a process, you are being guided by the shakti of Narayana, as he is the planner and the sustainer. You have to act according to Narayana in this life. According to the will of Shiva, you bring about change; and according to the grace of Narayana, you maintain, develop and beautify it. Therefore, this mahayajna, dedicated to Lakshmi and Narayana, is a stepping-stone in your spiritual journey. If you can understand it in the right manner, this yajna is a stepping-stone in your spiritual journey that will help uplift the state of your soul.

Open the heart and mind for divine grace

Every year at the yajna, some divine indication has taken place to signify the presence of Narayana. In the year 2011, with the first Lakshmi-Narayana Mahayajna, for the first time in the history of Munger, on the first day and on the last day, two deer were seen walking around the banks of the Ganga. Never before had those deer been seen in Munger and nor

have they ever been seen since. The only sightings were on the first and last day of the yajna in 2011. Lakshmi and Narayana had come in the form of deer to see their yajna, and where they went after that nobody knows.

That same year, Garuda, the vehicle of Narayana, came and did one parikrama before the yajna began, during the procession when Narayana came to take his place. On the last day too, when Narayana left, the *garuda* or eagle came, did a parikrama, then flew over the Ganga and disappeared in the distance, as if the program was over and it had to go.

In the other yajnas also, many different omens have been witnessed. Similarly this year, special visitations have taken place. Many eagles have come to Ganga Darshan and to Paduka Darshan to ensure that the preparations are happening in the right manner. These eagles are watching everyone keenly. Through their keen vision, they are observing everyone. If you are the right one, you will be the recipient of grace; if you are the wrong one, you will go back empty-handed. If your thought is the right side up, then it can be filled with grace. However, if your head, your pot, is turned upside down then grace will simply fly over it and your pot will remain empty. You must decide whether you want to be the recipient of the grace or whether you want to go back empty-handed. You will receive what is due to you according to the choice you make, and you will either receive in abundance or nothing at all.

Each one receives what is due to them: nothing extra, nothing more and nothing less. Nonetheless, do not worry about what you are going to get or not going to get. Try to know how you can become a better recipient by opening your heart and mind. If you can open your heart and mind and keep it open, then grace will fill your cup. If you are unable to open your heart and mind, nothing can be received. The attempt and effort has to be in opening your heart and mind during this program.

Be quick, be creative, be peaceful, be silent and enjoy

Narayana gets angry, Shiva gets angry and even the guru gets angry. The guru's systems and disciplines are not normal systems and disciplines. The guru's systems and disciplines are strict, and you all must follow them. Otherwise, chain reactions happen. Follow the system properly and be quick in what you do. Follow a simple sutra: 'What you can do tomorrow, do today and what you can do today, do now.' If you follow this sutra, you will be successful.

Some people work as if they have the entire week to decorate. No. Finish your work in half an hour and leave. Do something else. Do your things quickly and be ready to sit down. When you have nothing to do, sit down, enjoy yourself and participate; open yourself. When you have something to do, complete it in the shortest time possible, without wasting time. That is your training.

Bring forth your creativity and do things properly in the right manner. This is your sadhana as well: to be able to be creative, peaceful and quiet. Let your actions show how much you have gained through your meditation in this week. Show through your actions what you have achieved in life. Participate whole-heartedly in this Lakshmi-Narayana Mahayajna and receive the divine grace. Be innocent, be simple, be pure, be active, be creative, be fast, be dynamic, be peaceful, be happy, be joyous, and enjoy.

Close the kitchen to receive Narayana's mahaprasad

How many of you have heard of Jagannath Puri? It is a famous temple of Lord Jagannath. *Jagannath* means the Lord of the universe: *jagat*, universe, and *nath*, lord or master. Jagannath Puri is the centre of Narayana. We sent an invitation to the temple and invited Narayana to come to this program. He said, "I will definitely come, but I want to do something for all of my people who are going to be there." We asked him, "What are you going to do for us, O Lord? We are doing this for you. What are you planning for us?" He said, "I have already instructed my cooks at the temple to send prasad from Puri, Orissa, to Munger."

The prasad from the temple will reach Munger tomorrow. We shall all be having the prasad that has been sent from Jagannath Puri and our kitchen will be closed. For the first time in the history of the ashram, its kitchen will remain closed during a program. Narayana is going to take care of the kitchen and the cooking. What a beautiful way to start!

When you receive that food tomorrow, receive it as prasad and then it will have meaning for you. Receive it as a divine blessing, not as rice and dal that you may or may not like. Likes and dislikes are your taste and your senses, and senses always lead one into trouble. I have never seen any sense leading anyone in the right direction so far. All the senses lead people down the wrong path, as they are extroverted, external and materialistic. Receive the meal as prasad from God, with all your heart, and then it will have value and meaning. If you receive it as food coming from Orissa, from some temple that you do not know and you do not care about, then that food will not nourish you and you will not be the recipient of divine grace.

Have faith: Narayana feeds all

One day in heaven, Lakshmi was searching for Narayana, "Where is Narayana, where is he?" Without informing Lakshmi, Narayana had disappeared from the house and so Lakshmi became worried. She searched every room, "Where is Narayana? Where is Narayana? Where is Narayana?" yet she could not find him in the flat. She became worried and dialled 911, "Heavenly police! I can't find Narayana! Where is he?"

Once heaven's 911 was dialled, all the gods started to search for Narayana and they found him walking along a small footpath on his way back home. They asked him, "Where had you gone?" Narayana said, "I was doing my duty." "What is your duty?" they asked. "Well, I have to sustain life. I have to feed the people. I have to make sure that everyone in this world is fed." Lakshmi started to laugh. She said, "You mean that you feed everybody, including the birds and the insects as well?" Narayana said, "Yes." Lakshmi said, "All right, I am happy to hear that," and she hatched a plan in her mind.

The following night, while Narayana was asleep, Lakshmi went out and caught an ant. She put the ant in a metal box, buried the box in the soil, stamped on the soil, then left to go to sleep, leaving the box with the ant inside. The next morning, Narayana disappeared once again; however, this time Lakshmi knew that he had gone to feed all of creation and she waited at home. When Narayana came back, Lakshmi taunted him. "Have you fed everybody in this creation?" Narayana said, "Yes." "All the birds?" she asked. "Yes," was the reply. "Reptiles?" "Yes." "Insects?" "Yes." Lakshmi said, "Today I am going to prove you wrong. There is one life form that you have not fed." With that, she went into her garden, dug up the ground, took out the metal container, took it to Narayana and said, "Inside this metal container is a creature that you have not fed."

Narayana said, "Show me." She opened the container and inside was the ant, sitting happily with a piece of sugar in its hands, eating it. So even when Lakshmi tried to hide a life form from Narayana, Narayana provided it with a grain of sugar to eat.

Now imagine, Narayana, the one who feeds the entire creation including every insect and every ant, is sending us his prasad, food that has been cooked for him. He said, "This prasad goes to Munger." You are the lucky ones to receive it tomorrow. What a beautiful way to kick-start our Lakshmi-Narayana Mahayajna, with the grace of Narayana and with food blessed by Narayana!

Propitiating Narayana

Swami Niranjanananda Saraswati
8 September 2013, Morning

Welcome to all of you on the first day of the Lakshmi-Narayana Mahayajna. The impersonal, invisible, universal, cosmic consciousness, which in broad terms is named God, has three main aspects. The first aspect of God is creation. Creation cannot happen without understanding and knowledge, without processing the experience, without processing knowledge. In this way, creation and knowledge become the first attribute of this Cosmic Self: the concept of Brahma and the concept of Saraswati.

Once creation has taken place, the second aspect becomes more important: to nurture, protect, preserve, sustain, maintain and provide opportunities to evolve, develop, grow, progress and be prosperous in life at all levels and in all dimensions. This second aspect of the Universal Self is known as Narayana and Lakshmi. The third aspect is Shiva and Shakti, the aspect that brings change. This aspect changes the manifest that has been created to allow options to develop and create something new.

Brahma and Shiva are responsible for your birth and death, and it is Narayana who is responsible for your life. From the moment you are born until the moment you take your last breath, you are under the control and jurisdiction of Sri Narayana and his consort, Lakshmi. Narayana is the sustaining power of life. Narayana is consciousness. Narayana is 'sentient-ness'. Lakshmi is prosperity; the fulfilment and the contentment that you experience when there is nothing lacking, when there is no vacuum in your life, when you are full. Then you become whole. The Lakshmi-Narayana Mahayajna is the opportunity to invoke this living principle of life in the form of Sri Narayana.

Creation is Narayana

Om sahasra sheershaa purushah. Sahasraakshah sahasrapaat.
Sa bhoomim vishvato vritva. Atyatishthadda shaangulam.
Purusha evedagvam sarvam. Yad bhootam yachcha bhavyam.

There is an entire *richa*, an entire poem, the *Purusha Suktam*, dedicated to Sri Narayana describing him as the life force with a thousand heads, a thousand arms and a thousand feet, indicating that he is innumerable. Anything that is perceivable is Narayana. Anything that is growing is Narayana. Anything that is content is Narayana. Anything that is developing is Narayana. The whole of life is Narayana. The whole world is Narayana: *Jale Vishnu sthale Vishnurvishnuh parvatamastake* – "This entire creation is Narayana." When you invoke this sustaining power it fills you internally. It makes you rich materially and spiritually. It makes you content: socially, emotionally and mentally. You become fulfilled.

Enticing Lord Narayana's presence

This yajna was the mandate given to Sannyasa Peeth by Sri Swamiji in the year 2009 when he passed on the responsibility to fulfil this third vision of his life. At that time, as his blessing he had said to me, "Invoke Lakshmi-Narayana." Since the first year in 2011, every time this event has been celebrated, special benedictions have been felt by everybody present. Unique visions have been seen by many participants. Unique omens have been experienced by many present, and many lives have been touched by their participation in this yajna.

It is a special yajna, coming to us with the blessings of a siddha guru, Sri Swami Satyananda, and carrying his sankalpa and his wish for all of us. Furthermore, due to his sankalpa and his wish, and our conviction and dedication to this sankalpa, even Lord Narayana becomes present during this time. Another reason why Narayana has to be present is that today the birthday of our paramguru and future guru too, Swami Sivananda, is being celebrated. His first birthday is being celebrated and he is turning one year old, so to have a fitting celebration Narayana has to appear.

Narayana has been encircled from all sides. Swami Sivananda's birthday; the gathering of such beautiful people; the sankalpa of a sannyasi; the presence of competent acharyas; and the presence of so many flowers that make the garden look so colourful and beautiful: these are all enticements for him. Every year the effort is made to make this place more beautiful so that one day he can say, "I am not going back to my dimension. I am going to stay here for all times to come."

Ganapati Bapa Morya

Swami Niranjanananda Saraswati
9 September 2013, Morning

An auspicious beginning

Today is the second day of the Lakshmi-Narayana Mahayajna and it is also Ganesha Chaturthi. The first day of the yajna was very auspicious. In the morning I received a phone call from Swami Satyasangananda, the peethadhishwari of Rikhiapeeth, and she said, "We have just completed our program." I replied, "Yes, and we have just started our program." The conclusion of Rikhiapeeth becomes the beginning of Sannyasa Peeth. Also, the first birthday of Paramguru Sri Swami Sivananda was celebrated with a beautiful dance drama last night that depicted his entire life and teachings, and which was most inspiring and uplifting.

On top of that, to crown the first-day celebrations and the beginning of the Lakshmi-Narayana Mahayajna, when Lord Jagannath from Puri was invited to come to this yajna, he said, "I will come, but I will also take up another responsibility, and that responsibility is that I will feed everyone who is in Munger." True to his word, cars and trucks rolled in yesterday to the main gate, along with the chanting of mantras, and brought in happiness.

Yesterday our kitchen was closed and Lord Jagannath opened his kitchen. Not only the people here who were present in the program received the prasad; many people in the town also received the prasad of Lord Jagannath. He kept his word that, 'I will come and I want to feed the people of Munger. That is my responsibility.' That is the beauty of Jagannath. I told you the story of the ant and the grain of sugar, and how Narayana, how Jagannath feeds each and everyone. This feeding is physical, it is internal, it is spiritual, and it is the experience of atman. It is this nourishment that gives us the experience of life.

Last evening we also witnessed a beautiful Odissi dance performance, which is traditionally performed at the Jagannath temple in front of the Lord. The person who performed this dance did not learn it from a teacher; and instead she learnt it by downloading clips from the internet and copying the steps. It is just coincidence that everything has happened in this manner: that the prasad was received, Lord Jagannath came, the temple dance was performed, his grace was received, Swami Sivananda's celebration was conducted, the beautiful dance-drama was enacted and the beautiful commencement of the program took place here. Furthermore, until the day before yesterday, it was impossible to sit here for five minutes, even in the coolest shade. Then yesterday the entire climate and winds changed and today you are able to sit here. Yesterday you sat here for the whole day without feeling any discomfort. This is an indication of the presence and grace of Paramguru Sri Swami Sivananda, of Sri Swamiji and of Lord Narayana and Lakshmi who are here in Munger today.

Celebrating Ganesha Chaturthi

The next part of the program will be cracking the coconuts for the Ganesha pooja, which will begin soon to celebrate Ganesha Chaturthi today.

Instructions: This is the group that will be cracking the coconuts. The pandit has given specific instructions. He says if you are wearing a leather belt, remove it. Nothing leather except your own beautiful skin; keep what is natural to you, and keep aside what is not natural to you. Second, when you hit the coconut you have to break it in one go, in one stroke. You cannot break it in two strokes. It has to be one big one. Then pick it up immediately and if there is water in it, put the water in the container. It does not matter if some of the water falls out.

These are the two main rules of breaking the coconut that you have to remember. Each one of you will be called one by

one. When you are called, you will be purified by the water and you will be handed a coconut. When the *Swaha* is being said, you have to break the coconut on the stone; and do not worry about the stone, just try to break the coconut.

Conclusion: All the participants were like little children waiting to break their coconut. Some people had a soft touch. Some people had a sledgehammer touch. Not a single coconut was rotten. When you buy coconuts in large quantities, it is difficult to distinguish the rotten ones, yet not a single coconut was rotten.

Two different activities have been completed. While people were breaking the coconut with each *Swaha*, the pandits were offering a whole coconut into the fire. In the yajna vedi, havan was performed with the offering of a coconut and on the outside, a coconut was offered to Ganesha.

This has been the most unique Ganesha Chaturthi program.

Creating a beautiful garden of life

Sri Swamiji has said that if you have only one type of flower in a garden, then that garden may be nice; however, it is not attractive. On the other hand, if in one garden you have different varieties of flowers; some big, some small, some yellow, some pink, some blue, some magenta, all different colours; some with big leaves, some with small leaves, some with no thorns and others with thorns, then all the variety of plants that give flower beautify the garden. In the same manner, a human being is a collection of different thoughts, perceptions, ideas, traits, behaviours, mentalities, aspirations, nature and inclinations; which are actually a collection of flowers that are showing their beauty in your life.

If somebody is envious, then it is the flower of envy that is showing its beauty. If somebody is kind, then it is the flower of kindness that is showing its beauty. If somebody is angry, then it is the flower of anger that is showing its beauty. What you express is a creation of yours, and what you create is the flowering of your mind, your nature, your traits and your character. Therefore, a human being is like a collection or a bunch of flowers.

When you offer yourself, when you bow down in front of somebody, when you bow down in front of guru or God, the sentiment has to be that 'My life is a garden in which everything has grown, the beautiful and the ugly both, the green and the dry both. It is this garden of my life that I am offering to you, O my Lord. Accept it with all the flowers that it has.'

Ways to Remember

Swami Niranjanananda Saraswati
10 September 2013, Morning

Today is the third day of this Lakshmi-Narayana Mahayajna, although the yajna really started from the 5th. The period from the 5th to the 13th is celebrated as *Sumiran Saptah*, remembrance week. The remembrance week proceedings begin with two days of *aradhana* or worship in commemoration of the mahasamadhi and bhu samadhi of our guru, Sri Swami Satyananda. Every month on the 5th, a beautiful Rudrabhisheka is performed at Shiva Peeth in Satyam Udyan at Ganga Darshan; and every month on the 6th, two different

Sri Yantras are worshipped with abhisheka, one from the vedic point of view and one from the tantric perspective.

Then on the 7th in pratyahara and dharana we remembered Narayana and Lakshmi, keeping their memory alive all the time. That is the real yoga. It is said in a couplet:

Aisa jaapa japo mana lai, soham soham surata gai
Chhaisau sahasa ikkisau jaap, anahada upaje apai aapa.

In relation to yoga and to a specific technique of concentration called ajapa japa, Sage Kabir Das makes a pronouncement: "Fix your mind in such a way that your breath begins to sing the mantra *So-Ham*, *So-Ham* naturally

and spontaneously. When you can retain that span of awareness for twenty-four hours of the day or for 24,600 breaths, then you will realize the anahada, which is the source of all sounds."

What Kabir Das is speaking of as dharana, as a sadhana in the form of ajapa japa, is what we all practise in sadhana here at the yajna. The point of our dharana and our focus is Lakshmi and Narayana. Everybody who is here who thinks of this 'Lakshmi-Narayana dharana' is making a mental preparation for the yajna. This is a spontaneous form of yoga. You do not have to sit in isolation to remember somebody. Whom you remember is always there, present in front of your eyes; and that is the greatest meditation, the greatest dharana and the greatest pratyahara.

Tuning in to God's subtle wavelength

The Lakshmi-Narayana Mahayajna started on the 8th with the celebration of the first birthday of Paramguru Sri Swami Sivananda. This time a special blessing was also received. The ashram received food for everybody from Jagannath Mandir in Puri, Orissa. Mr Sharma, the person who brought the food here, was telling me yesterday that ten months ago he had a dream. At that time, he was not even connected with us. He did not know Swami Niranjanananda. He did not know Swami Satyananda. He did not know Swami Sivananda. He did not know Bihar School of Yoga. He did not know Munger. He did not know Rikhia. He did not know anybody. Yet, ten months ago, he had a dream that he was delivering some prasad to some place where bald-headed sannyasins were dancing. These bald-headed sannyasins were dancing, receiving and taking the prasad, which thousands of people ate. This was the dream he had ten months ago.

Then only ten days ago, a swami here came across him and mentioned the mahaprasad. When the man brought the mahaprasad here, he was stunned. He said, "This is what I had seen in my dream. It was this ashram. It was these people. It was this prasad that I was delivering!" He said that each driver – there was only a single driver in each car – drove for twenty-seven hours without stopping, without a meal break; they stopped only to relieve themselves and to drink some water. For twenty-seven hours continuously they did not break. Imagine that! This is not the US. This is not Europe. A single driver in India, driving for twenty-seven hours without food, without rest, with only one thought on his mind, 'The prasad has to reach there on time. The prasad has to reach there on time. The prasad has to reach there on time.' This is the blessing. The flags that came with them of Lord Jagannath from Puri have been put around Sri Narayana and Lakshmi.

Chanting the divine names

Today, in the morning session there will be a rendering of the stories of Narayana by Srimati Krishna Devi. Then in the afternoon session, the *sahasranama* will be performed, the chanting of one thousand mantras and the offering of a specific item to an image of Lakshmi and Narayana, which will be given to the people making the offering; one thousand times on behalf of Lakshmi and one thousand times for Narayana. That means those people will make two thousand offerings today. One thousand people have been selected. When you come here in the afternoon, you will find the plate and the items for offering, and the image of Lakshmi and Narayana ready, waiting for you.

Come in a dignified manner with reverence, respect, conviction and faith. Do not come chatting away, "Where shall I sit?" "You come and sit beside me." "Let us sit together." "Let us go here, let us go there." Stop all that. This is aradhana, worship, and an invocation. Invocation is avahan: 'I am calling you'; that is the meaning of the word 'avahan'. When we invoke a deity, we use the word *avahan*. When you do the *sahasrarchana*, the one thousand offerings, do it with reverence, respect, dignity, faith and conviction that the right thing will be done.

Thousands of Divine Offerings

Swami Niranjanananda Saraswati
10 September 2013, Afternoon

The program will now begin with the havan and the pooja of the pandits, and after that at four o'clock we shall begin the sahasrarchana.

With each swaha

Instructions: One thousand names of Lakshmi and one thousand names of Narayana will be chanted. With each name, first the offering will be made to Lakshmi with *kum kum*, red vermilion powder. Only a pinch needs to be taken,

between the third finger and the thumb; just a little pinch and put it on the yantra that will be given to you. Put one pinch of kum kum on the yantra with each mantra.

After the *Lakshmi Sahasranama* is performed, you will be given a piece of plastic. You will have to put the plastic on top of the kum kum and then we shall start with the *Narayana Sahasranama*, which will be performed with tulsi and with grains of rice. Only the third finger, that is the ring finger, and the thumb are used. Pick up one or two grains of rice and put it on the yantra. Not a handful, just one grain is enough. One grain or two grains of rice, one tulsi leaf and one pinch of kum kum.

Take the blessings with you

Conclusion of sahasrarchana: It is written that whenever an auspicious activity comes to its conclusion and has fructified, you will know that it has been accepted by the arrival of a saint. As we concluded the sahasrarchana, our own Swami Satsangi, the peethadhishwari of Rikhiapeeth appeared in our midst. Let us welcome her.

We have concluded a special program, Swami Satsangi. One thousand people here today have done sahasrarchana, first to Lakshmi with kum kum and then to Narayana with tulsi and rice. They have received a thali with a symbol of Lakshmi and Narayana on one side and a Sri Yantra on the other side. This they will take back with them.

Everything that is in front of you, you may take back with you. It is for you, for your family and your community, as the grace and the blessings of this Lakshmi-Narayana Mahayajna, as the blessings of Sri Swamiji and the blessings of Sri Swami Sivananda.

Now we will start the Ganga arati, the arati to Mother Ganga.

Lord Narayana in Yoga Nidra

Swami Niranjanananda Saraswati
11 September 2013, Morning

The children were narrating a story that reminded me and brought to the surface old memories of Sri Swamiji. The children were recounting how Narayana reclines on his bed of serpents with his eyes closed in yoga nidra and he never sleeps, and Lakshmi is there with him all the time. Although his eyes are closed, Narayana is always awake. There is no sleep for Narayana. The sustainer of life will not sleep. He can close his eyes; however, he cannot go into a slumber. The moment he goes into a slumber, life will stop. If life in your body goes into a slumber, what will happen? You will cease to exist. Therefore, Narayana never sleeps.

What does he do to compensate for this lack of sleep? He practises yoga nidra. *Yoga nidra* is a sleepless sleep in which you are supposedly sleeping, however, internally you are awake, alert, conscious and in full control of the faculties. This is the state of Narayana too, the *Narayana vritti*: always alert, always conscious. Even though the senses may be shut off, cut off, closed and dormant, the mind and the consciousness become the witness and observe everything, as if watching everything with the eyes open.

Sri Swamiji's Narayana vritti

The story that the children told reminded me that in all my time with Sri Swamiji, I have never seen him sleep. I spent fifty years of my life with him. I have spent all my life with him, sometimes close to him, sometimes far away, sometimes in the same room, sometimes in different capacities and in different conditions. In all that time I have never seen him sleep. No. The lights may be off, the doors may be shut, yet if you make a single noise, a single sound, if you drop a needle, choose your time: 12 o'clock, 12.30 am, 1 am, 2 am, 3.30 am, the sound that the needle make will evoke a response from Sri Swamiji, "What is it? Who is there?" That was his type of his relaxation, always in a state of yoga nidra.

Many people have spent sleepless nights trying to record a snore or the sound of deep breathing to see if Sri Swamiji did ever sleep, however they have failed, and sitting here today they still wonder whether Sri Swamiji ever slept or not. This is the reality that we have witnessed. I am not telling you an imaginary story or creating a fantasy. No. A single noise, one single movement would evoke a response from him at any given time, when people are supposedly fast asleep in the lap of Mother Earth and unconscious.

The children's message is that Sri Swamiji was filled with the Narayana vritti. He gave us the message to love, to live and to laugh. He always stayed in the state of yoga nidra, and his parting gift to all of us was the gift of yoga nidra, which is what Narayana does all the time.

God is the Only Reality

Swami Niranjanananda Saraswati
11 September 2013, Afternoon

Today concludes the fourth day of the Lakshmi-Narayana Mahayajna. The Lakshmi-Narayana Mahayajna begins on the 8th of September, the birthday of our paramguru, Swami Sivananda. This year, everybody experienced beautiful grace in the form of Lord Jagannath's prasad all the way from Puri, Orissa. The whole event was not known to us until about ten days ago; however, the vision that the event would happen was seen ten months ago by the person who brought the prasad. This was a most special and unique event. God knew ten months ago what he was planning to do, and we came to know only ten days ago that something is possible. That is the difference between what God has planned and what a human being thinks. This has been a most special event on the occasion of this Lakshmi-Narayana Mahayajna. The flags that came from the Jagannath Puri temple have been placed around Lakshmi and Narayana. In this way the grace of Lakshmi-Narayana is here in abundance.

The catalyst, the one who brought this grace down to our level, is none other than our own guru, Sri Swamiji. To give this Lakshmi-Narayana Mahayajna as prasad to people who participate here was his instruction, guidance and direction to Sannyasa Peeth. The prasad of Shakti and Shiva during the Sat Chandi Mahayajna and the Yoga Poornima Mahamrityunjaya Homa, the prasad of Sri during Akshaya Tritiya, the prasad of Lakshmi-Narayana during *Sumiran*

Saptah, the week of remembrance: these are events that have happened naturally and spontaneously, and they convey the sankalpa of Sri Swamiji and the grace of God.

Seeing the divine spark in all

Prior to his mahasamadhi, Swami Sivananda went into a clinically-unconscious state. 'Clinically unconscious' means coma, yet yogically he was not in a state of coma. Yogically he was in a state of samadhi. After twenty-one days he came out of that state and uttered only one sentence, "God is the only reality, surrender to it." This was the final statement of Paramguru Swami Sivananda, his final teaching and instruction.

As long as Sri Swamiji was working to establish yoga as a science, a subject, a way of life, a philosophy, a system of thought, a practice and a sadhana, he steered away from the subject of bhakti and God. Although he was the greatest bhakta, he never spoke publicly on this subject. When he went to Rikhia, however, he spoke on it freely and openly.

Sri Swamiji says everybody should cultivate a relationship with the Higher Self. Everybody should cultivate *atmabhava*, an ability to see the higher nature, the divine nature in each and every thing. Just as you see yourself reflected in your people, in the same manner see the reflection of God, the divine Self, the transcendental Self in each and everyone. A thirsty person is also a reflection of a thirsty God. A hungry human being is a reflection of a hungry God. A sad human being is a reflection of a sad God. A happy human being is a reflection of a happy God. Discover that. See that in everyone. See that essence; see that presence, see that power in everything and everyone.

Today as we sit here in this place of aradhana and avahan, we realize that something is present amongst us, whether you call it a feeling, a vibration, the cool breeze on a hot summer's day, or the quenching of thirst if you are absolutely parched and dry. Whatever brings relief to your system, body, mind and spirit indicates the *shakti* or the power of God. We are certainly feeling that, as many things have happened in this yajna. Omens have been in abundance to indicate that something extraordinarily special and auspicious is happening.

Calling out to the divine through yajna

All the parts of the yajna have been fulfilled. Yajna is *aradhana*, worship. Worship of what? It is the worship of life. It is the worship of atma. It is the worship of spirit. And yajna is not only a worship of life, atma and spirit, it is also an invocation; you are calling somebody.

When you call out somebody's name, "Come here, come here, come here quick", they come. If you simply say something to the air, nobody will come. By calling out someone's name, though, and by saying, "You! Please come here," they are compelled to get up and to walk this way. That is known as avahan. Avahan means I am calling you, "Come

here, please get up and come here." Aradhana and *avahan*, worship and invocation, are the components of a yajna. Yajna also has subcomponents:

Mantra: The sound vibrations that are being chanted.

Creation of yantras: Different yantras are created with rice, with different colours, and they represent the seat on which the deities can be invoked.

Mandala: Similarly, with the invocation of the mantras and the cosmic energies on the yantras, a mandala is created. A field or aura, a positive aura, a benevolent aura, a benevolent shakti is generated. That mandala is enforced with the positive intention, sankalpa and willpower of everyone.

Kirtan: Remembrance of God's name is part of the yajna.

Satsang: The purpose of satsang is to continuously, time and again, pull your awareness and your attention to the object of concentration, adoration and worship, so that you remain focused.

Gifting: To share, to give, to distribute the happiness, the auspiciousness and the bounty of yajna through the prasad being given is another aspect.

Dance: When people forget themselves, the body begins to dance by itself, too. When you remember yourself, then the body becomes still and stiff. When you forget yourself, then the body begins to dance at its own rhythm and pace. This was visible during the program. Those people who were conscious of themselves were sitting, and those people who had forgotten about the body and themselves were standing and dancing. If you become too self-conscious, then you become rigid and you will sit. If you simply flow with the current of God's name, then you can forget yourself and the body begins to sway to the divine rhythm by itself. You do not even have to make the effort.

Parting gifts of divine grace

Tomorrow this yajna will be concluded with the celebration of Sri Swamiji's sannyasa day. The yajna will conclude in the morning, and in the afternoon, a special sannyasa day program will be conducted in Paduka Darshan and then a special program in the evening at Ganga Darshan. With that, the Lakshmi-Narayana Mahayajna will be concluded. When we go, we shall go with the memory of Lakshmi and Narayana in our minds and in our hearts, and we shall go with the name of guru on our lips. We shall go with happiness and good wishes shared by everyone towards each other.

Satyam Vatika darshan: dedication of a disciple

Evening program: Satyam Vatika is the place that depicts the inspiration of Ganga Darshan. To fulfil the mandate of his guru, to live only by the command of his guru, Sri Swamiji set aside all his personal aspirations, ideas and thoughts. Satyam Vatika represents his *samarpan*, his one-pointed dedication and devotion to his guru, Sri Swami Sivananda.

Satyam Vatika contains statements and sayings by Sri Swamiji, as well as our paramguru, Sri Swami Sivananda, inspiring people to lead a life dedicated to service and a life dedicated to the divine. Each panel is an inspiration as it conveys the thoughts and the visions of our guru, Sri Swami Satyananda and our paramguru, Sri Swami Sivananda. When you go there, you are surrounded by the sankalpas of the two luminaries of this age. Let their sankalpas soak into you. May you live those sankalpas in the course of your life.

Poornahuti

12 September 2013, Morning

Complete the journey

Swami Niranjan: This morning the final *ahuti*, the final oblation, will be offered amidst the chanting of mantras and stotras, and havan. Other activities will also be carried out simultaneously. In the afternoon, we will celebrate the *sannyasa jayanti*, the sannyasa birthday, of our beloved guru, Sri Swamiji. We know him as an incomparable sannyasin.

This identity of a sannyasin, his initiation into sannyasa, was given to him by our paramguru, Swami Sivananda, on this day in 1947. Therefore, today we remember the ideals of sannyasa that Sri Swamiji has lived. Today we also make a sankalpa, whoever we are, whether sannyasins or spiritual aspirants, to follow the path that our guru has walked upon, according to our capacity and our ability. Some may complete the journey and some may only complete two steps. Nevertheless, the journey has to be started. Today, the day he was given sannyasa, let us take the sankalpa to begin this unstoppable journey into the spiritual unknown where only *sat*, the truth; *chit*, the attainments of consciousness; and *ananda*, the bliss, remain.

Dawn of yajna

Swami Satsangi: We are all very privileged to be here on the banks of the Ganga to make our offering at the Lakshmi-Narayana Mahayajna. Yajna is an ancient rite from prehistoric times. You can say that yajna began with the discovery and the tending of fire. Yajna began at the moment that man first discovered fire. You can imagine how ancient it is. Fire existed even before man, but man became aware of fire at a certain moment in time, and yajna started from then. He began to make his offerings of grains and different materials, those which he considered most dear and precious, into the fire. He offered it with feeling and emotion, *bhavana*, and with devotion and surrender. He began to offer these into the fire as well, and that is how yajna developed.

Yajna is a universal concept and is related to each one of you no matter where you belong. It does not relate to your past, to your creed, to your gender, to your nationality, to your relations, to your beliefs and social system. Fire is a primordial instinct in you, which you are addressing through yajna.

Purpose of yajna

Yajna is comprised of three concepts. One is creation. Yajna is production, creation. Two, yajna is preservation: to nurture, nourish, make it grow and make it more bountiful. The third is distribution. First, to create something, to produce something; second, to make it more beautiful, more effective, more potent, more dynamic, more vibrant, with more light, with more knowledge in it; and third to distribute it to everyone. It is a market economy.

What does yajna do? It markets blessings to each and every home. This market economy is far-reaching, effective and guided by the rishis and munis. How do you send blessings to everyone? So many people need blessings. That is what we need. We all need blessings. I need blessings, you need blessings, he needs blessings, she needs blessings. Everybody needs blessings. There is nobody who does not need blessings, regardless of whether they are humans, animals, minerals or plants. Everything in creation needs blessings, needs to be nurtured, and needs to grow. That is what yajna does; it distributes blessings to everyone.

There are thousands of yajnas. This is the Lakshmi-Narayana Mahayajna. Narayana is the preserver, the nurturer, the one who nourishes. Lakshmi-Narayana stands for nourishment, nurturing. If you do not nourish and nurture something that is created, what will happen to it? It will disintegrate, rot and decay. All the effort that was poured into creating something will go to waste. Is that how you live life? Are your lives just going to waste? Something was created: you! And someone created that. That life was given to you as a gift. Is it going to waste? Yajna is a far-reaching concept. It addresses the universality in man. It addresses that universal seed, which is in each and every person.

Yajna: a transformative powerhouse

Yajna is also the tool given by Sri Swamiji for the future. He gave two tools: one is yoga and the other yajna, and they are both complementary to each other. They are not contradictory. They complement each other because yoga has an esoteric side and an exoteric side, and so does yajna.

Yajna has an exoteric side and an esoteric side. The *karma kanda*, the rituals, are the exoteric part of yajna. The inner experience, the inner transformation, the inner change that takes place in you is the esoteric side. Yajnas generate change and transformation, and that transformation will continue for the rest of your life. You will feel the transformative effect of the yajna which you are attending now.

This transformation is generated through mantras. Mantra is the sound principle. If a sound pervades deep inside you, if you hear something that is pleasing, you are immediately affected by that. If you hear something that is disgusting, which irritates you, at once you are affected by that. Even your salivary glands are affected by the sound of the name of the food that you like. If I say 'chocolate', immediately, the mouth will start watering. If I say you are like God, you feel so happy. If I say, "God, you are horrible, you are so disgustingly ugly, rude and arrogant", you are not going to like that and immediately you will have a reaction. You will be affected, and it will spoil your mood, maybe your whole day, maybe even a few days, a few months, a few years, maybe a lifetime.

You cannot take insults. You cannot take injury. You need transformation. There is nobody who can say that he does not need to transform the self, to refine his awareness and to refine the qualities of his mind from tamasic to rajasic to sattwic. There is no living creature who can say that. Man is endowed with speech and knowledge, and therefore has an option. Animals do not have that option. Minerals do not have that option. The rest of creation does not have that option. Only man has that option and these are the two tools for evolution, self-evolution, evolution of the individual: yoga and yajna.

Quest for inherent knowledge

It is a great privilege to be here at this time, at this moment of celebrating birth and sannyasa, as that is the journey of life, the destiny of life, the destiny of each one of us: knowledge. Sannyasa means knowledge, the pursuit of knowledge at the cost of anything. Even if I have to give up my home, my friends, anything, I can give it up because I want knowledge. The quest has to be for inherent knowledge. I want knowledge from within me to come out, to unfold, to reveal itself. After all, the knowledge you seek is in you, it is not outside. Knowledge is inherent; the seed is inherent. You only have to bring it out. You only have to clear and remove the layers, the veils, the tamas. This is what yajna does; the sound of the mantras pervades deep inside you, into the causal body, the *karana sharira*, and removes the veils.

You are not just a physical body. You are also a subtle body, you are also a causal body, and it is in the causal body that the impressions are stored. The impressions are stored there, and these mantras are effective in bringing those impressions to the surface and purifying the different layers of your existence, the different bodies that you embody. Whether you know that or not is a different matter, yet you do have these bodies. You have the koshas, the tattwas and the gunas. Everybody is rajasic, tamasic and sattwic. Everyone is made of the *pancha tattwas*, the five elements. You have five koshas, and you have to purify at each level. What is it that purifies at all levels, not just at the surface, not just superficially? You can all have one coat of paint and look good, however, what about the deeper levels, the deeper levels that are actually the stuff that you are made of? To reach there, it is yajna that is effective.

It is this tradition that is being revived. It is an ancient ritual that Sri Swamiji has revived in the same efficient, systematic, simple and effective manner as he revived the tradition of yoga. Sri Swamiji has given you many traditions, not just one. There have been umpteen traditions and one can tire of counting them: sannyasa, yoga, yajna, sadhana, paramahamsa, rishi parampara. He has given so many that one gets tired of counting. Each one of these traditions he has revived in his lifetime and brought out in a manner that is so appealing, attractive and effective.

With this, I wish the most abundant blessings of Sri Gurudev Swami Satyananda on this sannyasa diwas, to all present, to all of us, as he is a part of us.

Yajna: an exact science

Swami Niranjan: On the first day the different deities were invoked to intensify the power, the *shakti*, the vibration of the yantras to protect the place and to protect the people who are participating in the yajna. Today, they will all be released. The process of concluding the yajna begins by releasing the invoked powers. They will all go back to their *loka*, their dimension.

There is a sequence in all these events. It is a sequential enactment, a process in which all the wheels have to turn together. Spiritual sadhana, the practices of yoga, of tantra and the lifestyle described in the vedic traditions all indicate a process of living that transforms life. Transformation in life has to take place whether you like it or not. The bud has to come out of the shell and the shell has to be broken. If the shell breaks naturally, spontaneously, then the bud will also come out in a natural manner. However, if you try to break the shell to facilitate the growth of the bud, the bud will also die when the shell is broken.

In the same manner, the sadhanas and the bhakti indicate a sequential process that has to take place, otherwise the wheels will get jammed and the car will not move. If you see any mechanical object, for example the cogs on a wheel, they merge as they rotate, they give impulse to the one before and push it forward. In the same way, here also the systems, the mantras, the invocation, the discharge, the release of the powers have to follow a specific system and timing. These timings are known as muhurtas.

Muhurtas

A *muhurta* indicates a specific time when one can perform a specific act. It is determined by examining what the nature and the quality of the time is, according to the conjunction of the zodiac symbols; whether it is the period that one is in for the next fifteen minutes, half hour or for the next three or six hours. These muhurtas, these times as indicated by the planets, are conducive for a specific act.

When you perform the right act at the right time it will give fruits; it will give results, better fruits, better results, sweeter fruits, greater results. If you do the wrong act at the wrong time, nothing is going to grow. If you do the wrong act at the right time, it will have a specific type of impact on the human psyche, on the human mind. If you do the right thing at the wrong time, it will have another impact on the human psyche and the human mind.

Yajna is actually a science. It is not a religious event or celebration that people can do or modify according to their whim and choice. It has to follow a sequence, just like when you drive a car. You do not start your car with the handbrake on and with your gear in fourth. You do not press the accelerator and the brake at the same time. In order to make the car move, you naturally follow a sequence of events. In the same manner, it is important to follow the sequence in order to make the yajna propitious and beneficial, and for everybody to receive the grace, the prasad of the yajna.

Sannyasa Diwas of Sri Swami Satyananda

12 September 2013, Afternoon

Happy birthday to you
Happy birthday to you
Happy birthday Swami Satyananda
Happy birthday to you
Hip Hip Hooray!

Celebrating an enlightened being

Swami Satsangi: All good things have to come to an end and it is always nice when the end holds promise of new beginnings. That is how this aradhana has been, because this is not just a program, it is not just a shivir, it is an aradhana. Aradhana has a lot of power. *Aradhana* means to yearn, to pray for and to long for. Aradhana is when you call from the depth of your heart, from the depth of your soul. In aradhana, you do not just call through the mouth, the mind or the emotions; you call out from the depths of your soul.

Usually you call out from the depths when you are in difficulty. It is when you are in difficulty you call out from the depth of your soul and your prayers are answered. That is the power of that call. It is the calling. You have to call. If you do not call, you will not receive. You have to call out. This is precisely the theme of this aradhana that is being conducted to celebrate both the birth, the *janmotsav*, of Swami Sivananda, of a great enlightened being who illumined the path of many; and the sannyasa of Swami Satyananda, who worked tirelessly for the evolution of mankind. He worked tirelessly for that. He was totally dedicated, and still is totally dedicated to the evolution of mankind. This was his main teaching: that man has to live a type of life by which his evolution is started, accelerated, and enhanced.

Sri Swamiji's message on evolution through bhakti

Maybe you are not evolving at all. You are just stagnating. How to give it a push? Sri Swamiji gave two tools for that: one was yoga and the other was yajna. Both are tools of self-evolution by which you can evolve your awareness. There are two processes of evolution going on in each person: one is evolution of mind and the other is evolution of awareness. They are different. They are not the same thing. The mind is evolving through your interaction with the world. You are becoming more intelligent, more intellectual; however, are you becoming more spiritual? That is the evolution of awareness. When you awaken to the reality and to the existence of something that you did not even know existed, and that exists within you, this is what he termed as 'evolution'. It is not a question of becoming good, better or more efficient. No, it is a question of your evolution, movement, growth and development.

Sri Swamiji said that the basis has to be *bhakti*, devotion. Bhakti is the medium by which you can practise the esoteric part of yajna or yoga. Bhakti has to be the medium. By bhakti he did not mean religion, where you go to the temple or you cry before God. No. By bhakti he meant a state of awareness, just as anger is a state of awareness. When you are angry, you are in a state of awareness. When you are grieving, when you are stressed, when you are confused or agitated, these are all states of awareness. In the same way, you can have a state of awareness called 'bhakti'. It is a brainwave, a pattern of the brain. And it is so necessary to have this state of awareness.

It is with this bhakti that you can experience peace, and in order to progress peace is essential. Peace in society, peace in the nation, peace in the world, and most importantly peace within yourself, because you have to live with yourself despite all the noise around you and the noise within your own self. That is what Sri Swamiji taught us, the evolution of man and the two tools of yoga and yajna.

Sri Swamiji says that the future belongs to bhakti. It is through bhakti that the problems and difficulties that you are facing will be solved. There is no other way. When in society there has been unrest, agitation, absence of peace and an increase in restlessness, it is always the bhakti movement and the divine mystery of bhakti that has come to the rescue, because bhakti has the power to align your awareness in the right way.

Relevance of love and unity in practising yajna

This is what you have been doing and feeling from the 8th to the 12th. You have been aligning yourself to the transforming station. This was a transforming station here, generating the energy. You have been aligning yourself with that, you have been tuning yourself to that, and you have been creating the frequencies to align with the energy that has been generated here at this place, the transforming station, which is the yajna. Through that a process has started, because that energy has entered you, into your eyes, your ears, through your skin. It has entered your being, and that energy works its way into the subtle realms of your existence. That is the power which you have experienced here.

Along with yoga, yajna has to be practised with love. To experience inner awakening, a higher level of existence, and peace of mind, one of the prerequisites is to feel love, whichever experience helps generate that feeling. That is one of the greatest teachings that Swami Sivananda and Sri Swamiji gave to us: serve, love and give. Yoga, yajna, serve, love and give, because the energy that one generates and creates has to be used productively. It has to be used first of all for the benefit of others and not only for oneself. Whatever one earns should not be used only for oneself. To feel this unity is the principle of yoga.

Remembering with every breath

There are people born in history who will give you that experience. It is not just a question of words, of telling and feeling; it is about resonating. You understand, you like, you

accept, yet you do not experience. Experiencing is a different thing. Such a person was Sri Swamiji. He could give you an experience of a change in awareness just by his darshan or just by his remembrance. That is the focal point of aradhana: remembrance.

Remember, remember, remember with every breath. It is the easiest thing to do, because that is what you do all the time. Remembering all the time. You are remembering. What is the use in remembering? You do not have to do much; you just have to remember. All the time you are remembering. It is the yoga of remembrance, the highest yoga of Swami Sivananda, which he himself practised. It is the yoga Sri Swamiji practised, the yoga of remembrance.

You attach your mind to whatever you remember. The mind has enormous power. You can travel halfway across the world and back in half a second; that is the speed of mind. Sitting here, you can travel to every corner of the world and then come back in half a second; that is the power of mind, and that mind has to be applied, it has to be disciplined, otherwise what are we remembering?

You may be remembering something that is harmful to you; you may remember sickness, you may remember things that disturb your mind. That is what you are remembering. You remember the time when somebody insulted you, when somebody spoke ill of you or when somebody tried to harm you. That is what you remember from morning to evening. For twenty-four hours, you are remembering.

That remembrance has to be directed, it has to be disciplined, it has to be refined and it has to be utilized to just remember. That was the sadhana given to Sri Swamiji: 'Remember me with every breath.' When you remember something, that is nyasa. When you practise yoga nidra, you remember every part of your body; that is nyasa. *Nyasa* means consecration. You are consecrating every part of your body, you are divinizing it, you are energizing every part of your body and you are awakening every part of your body. Just by remembering you are touching it, you are energizing it.

A consecrated life

Sannyasa means total consecration. If you have ten thousand dollars and you give it in trust for the treatment of the blind, once the money has been given you cannot use it after that. Even if you need some money later on, you cannot take it back because you have consecrated that money; it is no longer yours, you are just a trustee. In the same way, sannyasa is a total consecration of yourself to the divine through the power of *tyaga*, renunciation; *vairagya*, dispassion or detachment; and *viveka*, discrimination.

This is the consecration that Sri Swamiji fulfilled on the 12th of September. It is the moment of surrender, which he called *samarpan diwas*, the moment when he surrendered. The moment of surrender, when you do not belong to yourself; your body, your mind, your speech, your thoughts, your actions, and your dreams as well are no longer yours! Even when you dream, when you are unconscious and sleeping, even at that time your awareness is so disciplined that it follows the awareness of the guru. That is the kind of disciple that Sri Swamiji was, that is the kind of guru that he was, just living by remembrance.

Sri Swamiji lived for others. One of his main qualities was that he always lived for others. He never lived for himself. From his birth to the moment he left his body, and even now and in the future, it was always for others that he lived. He perfected that art. He perfected that skill. He had that skill. He always thought of others, how to uplift others, how they could benefit from something that he could tell them. That is how he was born.

The second thing that was very special about him was that he always gave to whoever sought his help, and he continues to do that, without hesitation. He never thought that 'This person is good, this person is bad', 'This person is deserving, this person is undeserving', 'This person is a cheat' or 'This person is a saint'. He always helped the person who approached him for help, and continues even now. And not only help, instant help.

Instantaneously he helped the people who approached him. That help was always full of wisdom. It was not out of any great affection or any great sentiment. It is because in that moment when you were in dire need and you needed help, you called out to him, you remembered him. You touched your mind with his energy and you received that consecration.

Through remembrance you consecrate your mind to a divine power, a divine energy. This should be the state of mind in this type of aradhana. When you remember the energy, the field that you are trying to invoke, and you connect to that, then your awareness begins to become streamlined. These are the aspects of evolution that are generated by the power of remembrance, of aradhana.

Power and potency of remembering Sri Swamiji

In the remembrance there has to be yearning. When you love somebody, then you have a yearning. You yearn to meet that person, to speak to that person, to think of that person. There is a yearning, a feeling; an intensity, a longing. That intensity and longing has to come into remembrance; only then is it yoga, only then is it yajna. Yajna and yoga have to be performed to the depths of remembrance. When you remember with your heart, your heart calls out, your soul calls out, your self calls out. From the innermost depth of your being, you call out to remember. That is what he taught us and this has to be applied to life itself. Not just for one hour in a day, not just for fifteen minutes, but to life itself.

Life has to become a life of remembrance, remembrance of those things that bring auspiciousness toward you. If you want life to be auspicious, remember auspicious things. That is the importance of this day: to remember a person just a second of whose remembrance can give you enlightenment, joy, peace, knowledge, clarity and focus, and which can centre and balance you, remove your difficulties, the ones that are so deep in you, the ones that are an inherent part of you. Nothing is hidden from the sadguru. That is the quality of the sadguru.

A guru of the type that Swami Satyananda or Swami Sivananda was is a sadguru. The sadguru is an antaryamin. *Antaryamin* means he knows what is happening in the inner life of everyone; he knows the inner life of everybody. Such people can guide and shape destiny, even if they are not in their body because they are synonymous with awareness, deep awareness.

So this is not just an event, it is a moment in time, the *muhurta*, an auspicious moment or *mangala bela*, when we all as disciples gather here to remember Gurudev. May the intensity of our remembrance – its purity, longing, craving, yearning and love – result in satyam and be full of joy, bliss, *ananda*.

Namo Narayana

Song of Consecration

Take my life and let it be
Consecrated, O Lord, to thee.
Take my hands and let them move
At the impulse of thy love.
Take my moments and my days
Let them flow in ceaseless praise.
Take my feet and let them be
Swift and beautiful for thee.
Take my voice and let me sing
Always only for my king.
Take my lips and let them be
Filled with messages for thee.
Take my silver and my gold,
Not a mite would I withhold.
Take my intellect and use
Every power as thou shalt choose.
Take my will and make it thine,
It shall be no longer mine.
Take my heart, it is thine own,
It shall be thy royal throne.
Take my love, my Lord, I pour,
At thy feet its treasure store.
Take myself and I will be
Ever, only, all for thee.

Swami Niranjan: This was the sankalpa that was lived by our paramguru, Sri Swami Sivananda. He had consecrated his life to the will of the Divine. It was this sankalpa that was given to Sri Swamiji at the time of his sannyasa, and Sri Swamiji lived every word in total, one hundred percent. That is what made Sri Swami Satyananda a unique personality, whom a unique guru was able to mould according to his desire and wish.

The greatness of the guru can be seen or recognized by the way they have lived with their master. The greatness of guru is not recognized by the comments, splendour, and a large retinue of followers. It is how they have lived with their guru and how they have allowed the guru to mould their character, nature, form, personality and mentality. This level of dedication and surrender makes a disciple one with the guru and makes the disciple a reflection of the guru; the guru comes alive within the disciple. This is what we have seen in the life of our own guru, Sri Swamiji.

Incomparable disciple and sannyasin

Many people take initiation, yet by taking initiation you do not become a disciple. Discipleship is a sacred act. Discipleship is not a label that you put on your body to say that 'I am a disciple of this swami', 'I am a follower of that sannyasi' or 'I am the disciple of this sannyasi'. No. Discipleship is not a label, and if you believe that then you are not a disciple. Discipleship is allowing the guru to come alive within you. It is possible. To allow guru to come alive within you, you have to surrender everything, all your associations of the senses and mind, all your associations of emotions and all your hang-ups; and simply focus and merge your awareness and identity in that of the guru.

Sri Swamiji represents this ideal of discipleship. He did not take sannyasa on the eighth of September along with the other guru brothers. He took sannyasa alone that year on the twelfth. Swami Sivananda had called him on twelfth and said, "I'm going to give you sannyasa, with only one instruction: wear this cloth and this colour closer to your body than your own skin. Never take it off." Sri Swamiji followed this mandate, and never in his life did he choose, desire or even think to put on geru pants to merge with society like many other people do. For him, his guru's command and words were the last, the final and the foremost. Nothing existed either before or after them.

Sri Swamiji was not like most people. Most people are not able to become disciples at all. They are the slaves of their own ambitions and desires, and those people make the guru the slave, expecting the guru to fulfil all of their expectations and desires. They never think about what they can do to fulfil the expectations that the guru has of them. They never think that. Whether they are sannyasin disciples or grihastha disciples, the guru becomes a stone on which they trample to achieve what they desire in life.

They never look at the guru with the eyes of a disciple. They look at the guru with the eyes of one who demands. They demand affection and love, they demand succour from their illness and problems, or they demand kundalini awakening and spiritual realization. There is always some kind of demand placed on the guru, whether it is for the family or for the business. That is the kind of relationship people cultivate with their guru. The guru is never seen as the guru, rather he is seen as the fulfiller of people's demands. That is why people have not been able to understand the intimacy, closeness, efficacy, strength and cosmic bliss that exist in the relationship between guru and disciple. Just wearing geru and saying that you are initiated by a sannyasin is not enough. There has to be dedication. There has to be surrender. More than anything, there has to be an understanding of your discipleship: how you have to behave as a disciple.

Three qualities of discipleship

There are laws that govern the relationship between guru and disciple. It is not a relationship only of *Twameva mata cha pita twameva;* that is one aspect of it. At the same time, there has to be a proper understanding of your connection with the guru, without which you cannot advance in the relationship.

Obedience: The connection with the guru has to be understood by observing your level of obedience. Sri Swamiji never questioned, he never even thought of questioning or altering what his guru had said. Even if the sentence was grammatically wrong, Swami Satyananda would keep it, as they were the sentences, the words, the shakti of his guru. Those sentences became dear to him. He did not modify the sentences to change the English, to change the meaning like other people do. He became one with his guru; he identified himself with his guru.

Sri Swamiji did not become a director of his guru, like many disciples today who even correct their guru, "Guruji, you are doing this in this manner, do it in that manner." If they have that much *akkal* or intelligence, then they should become the guru. Why are they searching for a guru or trying to be a disciple of somebody? Akkal, intelligence, is not the criteria. A deeper understanding and connection is the criteria between guru and disciple, and Sri Swamiji lived that.

Implicit faith: When his guru said to Sri Swamiji, "Work hard and the light will shine from within you," that sentence was enough to launch Sri Swamiji on the path of karma yoga and seva. He never thought, 'When shall I learn the yogas? When shall I learn the mantras? When shall I learn the scriptures?' He just had implicit faith in what his guru had said and, remember, it is this implicit faith that ultimately gives benefits. Sri Swamiji understood the instructions of his guru and knew what he had to do. He never asked whether he should do any asana and pranayama, whether he should practise a mantra that somebody had told him to do, or whether he should do something that he had learned from before. No, nothing. There was no question.

Surrender: Sri Swamiji himself clearly says that the moment he laid his head at his guru's feet, his mind became vacant of all questions. There was no questioning any more; there was only surrender. There was only letting go. It is this quality of Sri Swamiji that has made him what he is today, so close and dear to all of us. Not intellectual prowess, not the ability of attraction and repulsion, not wisdom and not the content of his knowledge, rather it was this identification with his guru. There was no difference between him and Swami Sivananda. They both became one: one spirit with two different bodies in two different times. It was the same spirit.

Live the teachings truthfully

Sri Swamiji has said many times that it is possible to cultivate this type of relationship. How to cultivate this? Develop that connection and be sincere, be truthful in that connection. Sri Swamiji has given you the path. He has shown you the path. He has given you the message; you only have to replicate that, live that in your life. Living his message in your life is the biggest tribute that you can offer to Sri Swamiji and his memory in this world. Living the teachings and the messages of Sri Swamiji is the biggest tribute that you can offer to a person of his character and nature.

Today we offer our heartfelt sentiments, and feel happy and proud that yes, he is our guru. Go with the thought that 'I am proud to be his disciple, and I will make every effort and aspire in every manner possible to live up to the concept of discipleship that he has lived and the path that he has shown us.'

Hari Om Tat Sat

Lasting Impressions: Experiencing the Divine

A selection of impressions by yajna participants

We are one

I saw the beauty of the invisible net
connecting all the people,
creating the space
where life flows perfectly

Being at the right time
in the right place,
with the right people . . .

Receiving and offering the
right things, sentiments,
words and blessings.

—*Sannyasi Chittamurti, Sannyasa Trainee, Slovenia*

Power of bhakti

The experience of Lakshmi-Narayana was one of expansion of awareness of the power and subtlety of bhakti . . . The location of Paduka Darshan gave a very clear sense of the difference between western concepts of yoga and sannyasa.

—Sannyasi Purnadhara, Australia

Timing

A small stone creates waves which reach far, far away
A single action, attitude initiates effects which influence so many; now I experienced and really know why it is so important to listen to those who know, who can see and fly.

—Sannyasi Nadamani, Sannyasa Trainee, Bulgaria

Grace

Guru's grace is always present in presence and darshan. Grace is there equally for everyone. The experience of grace does not depend on personal interaction or attention.

—Swami Anandakumar, Australia

Blessings! Blessings!

In symbolic form, Ganesha stands for an auspicious start,
Shiva the destroyer of bad things,
Narayana the nurturer of body and mind, and
Shakti the upliftment aspect for individuals,
Which we receive in yajna with guru's grace.

—Sannyasi Satyapriya, Sannyasa Trainee, India

God is omnipresent

After many days of struggle and trials, a sense of victory and invocation manifested on the last day during the final kirtan, when the murtis had departed and I looked around in inexplicable joy to see Narayana smiling and shining forth from the eyes and hearts of everyone as one; a beautiful momentary glimpse of guru and God's benevolent grace, glory, fathomless bliss and pure love.

—Sannyasi Vijayashakti, Sannyasa Trainee, Australia

Soaked in blessings

Unusual for this time of the year, pregnant Mother Ganga still flowing at her highest points as if she personally wished to grace the occasion, to participate actively in it and bless us all, filling us with her pure, snowy, Himalayan energy . . .

The entire five-day program was scheduled in two sessions: 9–11 am and 3–5 pm. Thousands of people assembled daily during both the sessions. They came from different parts of India and many came from abroad also. A large number of them came from Munger and its surrounding areas. The pandits performed the necessary poojas, the yajna havans and aratis with appropriate mantras and stotras and prayers in both the sessions. Although

generally not understandable, the people enjoyed the aradhana with deep shraddha and bhakti. The rapt attention and silence on the part of the audience was exemplary. This demonstrated their total absorption in the entire process of the event. Many people sitting in the pandal could be seen in musing moods. A large number of people experienced the blessings of the gurus and different deities. This could be seen on their beaming, joyous faces.

The prema bhakti of Srimati Krishna Deviji launched everybody almost to the state of bhava samadhi. She is popularly known as 'manas kokila' and that was amply demonstrated by her enchanting singing and narration of some important points of the *Srimad Bhagavatam* and *Ramacharitamanas*. Pujya Swamiji himself was very impressed by her sweet and loving chanting, so much so that he left his seat and sat with the audience, just in front of her.

Kirtans by the children of the BYMM were so nice. Everybody spontaneously danced to the tune of words, spirit and rhythm of their kirtans. Chanting of the stotras by the residents was invigorating and uplifting. The very special aspect of the yajna was the inspiring satsangs by Pujya Swamiji and Swami Satsangi.

During this five-day period, the entire campus was saturated and flooded with the grace and blessings of the gurus and the deities. It was experienced by one and all. This certainly happens. Even if you are not aware of the positive forces permeating the environment, it still penetrates into your whole being. The medicine works, even if you do not know the composition.

Finally, the pandits bade hearty farewell to the deities they had invoked at the beginning of the yajna. Although the gods are omnipresent, their presence is especially and strongly felt in such an environment and on occasions of this type.

Of course such an intensity of energy cannot exist at any point of place for a very long time nor can the people withstand it. Therefore, they are released with due regards and respects. However, they leave behind bearable power, energy and blessings that help the people through the vicissitudes of their lives . . .

—Swami Gyanbhikshu, Ganga Darshan